中国交通名片丛书

EXPRESS IN CHINA

中国快递

中国邮政快递报社 编

人民交通出版社

北京

"快递小哥"工作很辛苦,起早贪黑、风雨无阻,越是节假日越忙碌,像勤劳的小蜜蜂,是最辛勤的劳动者,为大家生活带来了便利。

——2019年2月,农历春节来临之际,习近平总书记在北京市考察。在乘车返回的途中,他来到前门石头胡同的快递服务点看望仍在工作的快递小哥。

《人民日报》2019年2月2日01版

The express deliverymen work very hard, from dawn to dusk, rain or shine. They become even busier during holidays. Just like diligent little bees, they are the hardest-working people delivering convenience to everyone's life.

In February 2019, when the Lunar New Year was approaching, General Secretary Xi Jinping made an inspection tour in Beijing. On the way back, he called on an express delivery service outlet in Shitou Hutong, Qianmen, Beijing and visited the express deliverymen on duty.

People's Daily, February 2, 2019, Page 01

编辑委员会

名誉主任　马军胜
主任委员　曾军山
委　　员　黄国忠　林洪亮　魏际刚
　　　　　　　高洪涛　钟奇志　张水芳

编　写　组

主　　编　李隽琼
副 主 编　阴志华　王　毅
分章负责人
快 递 中 国　王洪磊　王　毅
和 合 融 通　任国平　戴元元
时 代 命 题　李隽琼　赵立涛
特邀翻译　王　龙
其他参编人　曹　丹

Editorial Board

Honorary Chair	MA Junsheng
Chair	ZENG Junshan
Members	HUANG Guozhong LIN Hongliang WEI Jigang
	GAO Hongtao ZHONG Qizhi ZHANG Shuifang

Compilation Team

Editor-in-Chief	LI Juanqiong
Deputy Editor-in-Chiefs	YIN Zhihua WANG Yi
Chapter Leads	
Express China	WANG Honglei WANG Yi
Harmony and Integration	REN Guoping DAI Yuanyuan
Era Proposition	LI Juanqiong ZHAO Litao
Translator	WANG Long
Other Participant	CAO Dan

前 言

2021年10月，习近平总书记在联合国第二届全球可持续交通大会开幕式上的主旨讲话中指出，新中国成立以来，几代人逢山开路、遇水架桥，建成了交通大国，正在加快建设交通强国。

今日中国，公路成网，铁路密布，高铁飞驰，巨轮远航，飞机翱翔，邮路畅通，高速铁路、高速公路、城市轨道交通、港口万吨级泊位等规模均跃居世界第一。中国高铁、中国路、中国桥、中国港、中国快递成为亮丽的"中国名片"。

在交通运输波澜壮阔的发展历程中，中国快递业跑出了加速度，业务量从"年均百亿件"增长到"月均百亿件"，其规模之大、网络之广、动能之足、链条之长、发展之兴，已成为中国快递鲜明的标志。中国快递从2014年突破100亿件开始，年业务量连续10年蝉联世界第一，2023年突破1300亿件，占全球快递总量的六成以上。每天有400多万名快递员奔跑在大街小巷、乡村阡陌，14亿人口年人均快递使用量达94件。中国快递保持稳健的增长势头，市场主体健康发展，生产能力快速增强，服务水平不断提升，有力支撑了经济社会发展。

我们编写出版《中国快递》一书的主要目的是以图文并茂的方式向读者展示世界上最具活力的中国快递市场。一个个小包裹跑出了加速度，折射出中国经济的韧性和活力。一条条快递路不仅消弭了偏远乡村与繁华城市的地域鸿沟，更是畅通了工业品下乡和农产品进城的渠道，缩小了城乡差距。当前，绿色低碳发展已成为推动中国快递可持续发展的核心动力，科技创新正在引领中国快递发展，无人机、无人车、智能仓储各擅胜场，中国快递已进入高质量发展阶段。

翻开本书，我们可以领略中国快递广阔的服务网络，穿越山河，无远弗届；我们可以感受中国快递链接千城百业、联系千家万户、连通线上线下，促进和合融通，万物繁盛；我们可以见证中国快递服务乡村、服务产业、服务社会、服务就业，无处不在，促进全体人民共同富裕；我们可以展望中国快递积极融入全球供应链，与世界相交、与时代相通，绘就人享其行、物畅其流的美好愿景。

奋进新征程，我们要坚持以习近平新时代中国特色社会主义思想为指导，深入学习贯彻习近平总书记关于交通强国的重要论述，继续埋头苦干、担当奉献，再接再厉、再立新功，奋力加快建设交通强国，努力当好中国式现代化的开路先锋，为强国建设、民族复兴作出新的更大贡献。

编者
2024 年 9 月

PREFACE

In October 2021, President Xi Jinping delivered a keynote speech at the opening ceremony of the Second United Nations Global Sustainable Transport Conference, pointing out that since the founding of New China, generation after generation of the Chinese people have worked in the spirit of opening roads through mountains and putting bridges over rivers, and turned China into a country with vast transport infrastructure. Today, Chinese people are redoubling efforts to build China into a country with great transport strength.

China has already built a huge network of highways, railways, ships, airplanes and express delivery routes. China ranks first in the world in terms of the scale of high-speed railways, expressways, urban rail transit, and ports with 10,000-ton berths. China's high-speed railways, roads, bridges, ports and express delivery have become shining "business cards of China".

In the magnificent process of transport development, China's express delivery industry has achieved remarkable acceleration, with its business volume soaring from "an average of 10 billion parcels annually" to "10 billion parcels monthly". Its immense scale, extensive network, abundant momentum, extended chain, and vigorous development have become distinctive hallmarks of China's express delivery industry. Since exceeding 10 billion parcels in 2014, China's express delivery industry has ranked first globally in annual business volume for ten consecutive years, exceeding 130 billion parcels in 2023, accounting for more than 60% of the world's total. More than 4 million delivery workers rush through the streets and alleys, as well as the country roads of villages and towns every day, delivering a total of 94 parcels per capita annually among China's 1.4 billion population. China's express delivery industry maintains a steady growth momentum, with market players developing healthily, production capacity rapidly enhancing, and service levels continuously improving, providing strong support for economic and social development.

Our main purpose in writing and published the book "Express in China" is to display the world's most dynamic Chinese express delivery market to readers through illustrations and texts. Each small package racing ahead reflects the resilience and vitality of the Chinese economy. The express delivery routes have not only bridged the geographical divide between remote villages and bustling cities but also smoothed the channels for industrial products to go to the countryside and agricultural products to enter cities, thereby narrowing the urban-rural gap. Currently, green and low-carbon development has become the core driving force for the sustainable development of China's express delivery industry; while technological innovation is leading its progress. Drones, unmanned vehicles, and smart warehousing work effectively in their respective fields, indicating that China's express delivery industry has entered a stage of high-quality development.

Through reading this book, we can appreciate the vast service network of China's express delivery industry, spanning mountains and rivers, reaching every corner of the country; we can feel how China's express delivery connects thousands of cities and industries, millions of households, and both online and offline worlds, promoting harmony, integration, and prosperity; we can witness how China's express delivery serves rural areas, industries, society, and employment, being ubiquitous and promoting common prosperity for all; we can envision China's express delivery actively integrating into the global supply chain, intersecting with the world and the times, painting a beautiful vision of people enjoying their travels and goods flowing freely.

As we embark on the new journey, we must adhere to the guidance of Xi Jinping Thought on Socialism with Chinese Characteristics for a New Era, thoroughly study and implement the important exposition of General Secretary Xi Jinping on building China's transport strength, continue to work hard, take on responsibility, redouble our efforts, and achieve new successes. We must strive to build China into a country with great transport strength, strive to be the trailblazer in China's modernization drive, and make new and greater contributions to building a powerful country and realizing national rejuvenation.

Editors
September 2024

目　　录

快递中国：无远弗届　　1　　Express China – Extending to Every Corner

引言　　4　　Introduction

转运中心　不舍昼夜　　6　　Transfer Center – 24 × 7 Operations

干线路由　纵横交错　　14　　Trunk Routes – Intersecting and Crisscrossing

末端　星罗棋布　　22　　Terminal Outlets – Spreading Across the Country

国际　网络畅联　　30　　International – Well-Connected Networks

规模　快速增长　　36　　Scale – Rapid Expansion

服务　无处不在　　44　　Services – Ubiquitous

和合融通：万物繁盛　　49　　Harmony and Integration – Prosperity for All

引言　　52　　Introduction

服务乡村　双向奔赴　　54　　Serving Rural Areas – Mutual Development

CONTENTS

服务产业 质效双升	62	Serving Industries – Enhancing Quality and Efficiency
服务社会 迭代升级	70	Serving Society – Iterative Upgrades
服务就业 民生之本	78	Serving Employment – Foundation of People's Livelihood

时代命题：美好日长　　85　　Era Proposition – Promising Prospects

引言	88	Introduction
智能引领 各擅胜场	90	Intelligence-Driven Development – Each Shining in Its Own Way
创新求变 改革图强	100	Innovate for Change – Reform for Strength
开放共享 守护美好	108	Openness and Sharing – Guarding the Future
只此青绿 山河无恙	116	Green Sustainable Development – Harmony with Nature

后记　　124
　　　　125　　EPILOGUE

EXPRESS IN CHINA

中 国 快 递

快递中国：无远弗届
Express China – Extending to Every Corner

跟着快递看中国
See China Through Express Delivery

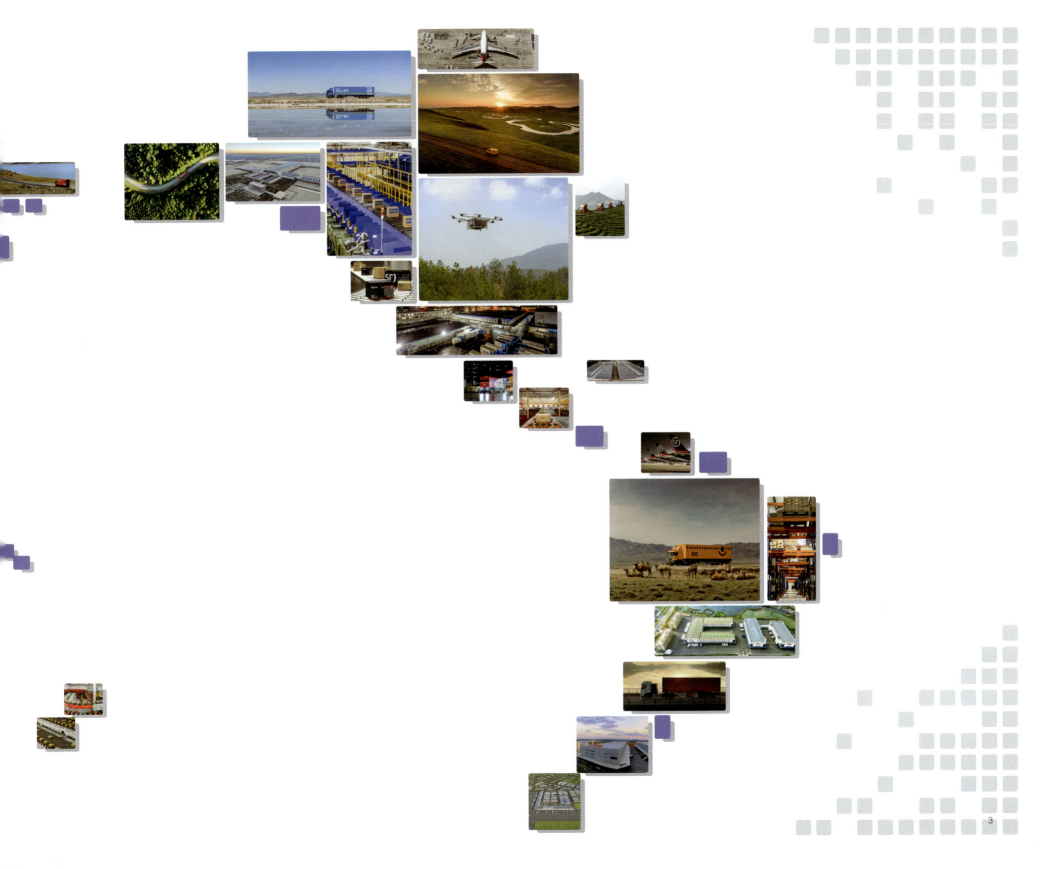

引 言

INTRODUCTION

从北国云天到南海疆域，从东海之滨到雪域高原，中国快递宛如无形的经纬，织就了一张世界上最大的快递服务网络。以星罗棋布的网点为基，以纵横交错的路网为络，这张网络不仅覆盖了中国广阔的疆域，更以绵延的力量触达世界的每一个角落。

在内蒙古广袤的草原上，当第一缕晨曦穿透薄雾，牧羊人指尖轻触手机屏幕，从千里之外订购的商品便悄然启程；在千帆竞发的南海之滨，渔民在晚霞映照下归航，他们捕捞的海鲜即可搭乘夜班飞机，穿越星辰，出现在远方百姓家庭的餐桌上；在遥远的西部戈壁，快递车辆穿行于风沙烈日，如现代版"骆驼商队"，为边陲送去美好和祝福。

在城市的高楼大厦间，一辆辆新能源电动车穿梭在繁忙的街道上，递送着来自五湖四海的包裹。在乡村的田野上，快递小哥背着包裹，奔走在蜿蜒的小路上，将乡村的新鲜与淳朴传递到四面八方。

中国快递网络的广阔，不仅仅体现在覆盖中国的深度，更体现在触达全球的广度。从欧洲的时尚之都，到美洲的繁华市区，再到非洲的新兴市场，中国快递公司的身影活跃其中，让"中国制造"走向世界的同时，也将世界各地的优质商品带回中国，展现出非凡的连接能力。

每一次网络的延伸，都是中国深化改革、扩大开放的生动注脚；每一处节点的构建，都是中国经济跳动的脉搏；每一个包裹的流通，都承载着与世界的共鸣之情。网络越来越大，世界越来越小。中国快递将中国与世界紧密相连，编织着一个更加紧密、包容、开放的全球经济新图景，书写着属于这个时代的繁荣新篇章。

中国快递，追求无远弗届。

Spanning from the northernmost reaches to the shimmering South China Sea, traversing the coastlines of the East China Sea and ascending to the snow-capped plateaus in the west, China has meticulously crafted the world's largest express delivery network. This intricate network, with outlets spreading all over China and an intricate system of interconnected routes, not only covers the vast expanse of China's territory, but also extends to every corner of the world.

As the first gentle rays of morning sunlight pierce through the misty veil over the vast grasslands of Inner Mongolia, a shepherd's effortless tap on their mobile screen initiates a journey for goods ordered from afar, embarking on a silent odyssey across thousands of miles. Meanwhile, on the busy coast of the South China Sea, as fishermen make their way home beneath the golden glow of sunset, the fresh catch they've reeled in hastens to board a nocturnal flight, destined to grace the dinner tables of distant households the very next day. In the remote and unforgiving Gobi Desert region in the west, express vehicles brave the unyielding winds, shifting sands, and scorching sun, reminiscent of a modern-day "camel caravan", delivering joy and blessings deep into the heartlands of the border regions.

Amidst the towering skyscrapers in the cities, new energy electric vehicles gracefully navigate busy streets, delivering parcels from all over the country. In the countryside, couriers traverse winding paths, carrying parcels that embody the freshness and simplicity of rural life to far-flung regions.

The vastness of China's express network is not only reflected in deep and extensive coverage in China, but also in its global reach. From fashion capitals of Europe, to vibrant metropolises of America, and even the burgeoning markets of Africa, you could find always the presence of Chinese express delivery enterprises. They are not only delivering products "Made in China" to the world, but also bringing high-quality goods from all over the world back to China, exemplifying an unparalleled capability to connect cultures and economies.

Every extension of the network is a testament of China's commitments to reform and opening up. The construction of every node resonates like a pulse, driving the vitality of China's economy. The circulation of every package carries a harmonious vibration that echoes throughout the world. As the network is getting bigger, the world is getting smaller. China's express delivery industry has intricately woven China into the fabric of the global economy, painting a vivid portrait of a closer, more inclusive and open global economy, and composing a new chapter of prosperity for this era.

China's express delivery extends to every corner of the world.

| 中国快递 | EXPRESS IN CHINA

转运中心 不舍昼夜
Transfer Center – 24×7 Operations

▼ 中国快递的发展得益于其庞大的市场规模、技术创新和基础设施建设等。图为夜幕中的中通快递转运中心。
The rapid development of express delivery industry is attributed to our huge market scale, technological innovation and infrastructure development. The picture shows ZTO Express' transfer center at night.

▲ 遍布各地的转运中心保证了每一件快件的准确送达。图为京东物流在江苏昆山的亚洲一号智能产业园。
Transfer centers all over the country ensure accurate delivery of each express parcel. The picture shows JD Logistics' Asia No. 1 Intelligent Logistics Park in Kunshan City, Jiangsu Province.

　　转运中心是快递网络的中枢神经，通常设立于城市边缘或是交通枢纽核心地带，快件在此汇集、分拣、重新启程。通过先进的自动化设备操作，每一份包裹都能准确无误地到达目的地。夜幕下，灯光璀璨，转运中心依旧忙碌，仿佛永不休眠的灯塔，照亮着每一件包裹流转的轨迹。

The transfer center is the central nerve of the express delivery network, strategically positioned on the fringes of a city or at the epicenter of a transportation hub. Here the express items are converged, sorted and distributed. Through the operation of advanced automation equipment, each package can reach its destination swiftly and accurately. As night falls and the lights on, the transfer center remains abuzz with activity, like a beacon that never slumbers, illuminating the journey of every package.

| EXPRESS IN CHINA

◀ 每一件包裹都会在这里留下存在的轨迹。图为圆通速递在广东虎门的转运中心。
Every package will leave a trace of its existence here. The picture shows YTO's transfer center in Humen, Guangdong Province.

▶ 每一个转运中心都见证着中国经济跳动的脉搏。图为韵达速递在浙江台州三门的转运中心。
Every transfer center is witnessing the beating pulse of China's economy. The picture shows Yunda's transfer center in Sanmen, Taizhou City, Zhejiang Province.

▲ 快递网络越广,世界变得越小。图为申通快递上海总部。
The bigger the express delivery network gets, the smaller the world becomes. The picture shows the headquarters of STO Express in Shanghai City.

▶ 傍晚的转运中心内即将迎来一天中最繁忙的时刻。图为极兔速递在湖南长沙榔梨园区中的转运中心。

The transfer center is about to usher in its busiest time of the day, as evening draws near. The picture shows J&T Express' transfer center in Langli Industrial Park, Changsha County, Changsha City, Hunan Province.

中国快递在陆上和空中织就了一张庞大的快递服务网络。图为夜色中的广东深圳宝安国际机场顺丰速运航空基地。
China's express delivery industry has woven a huge express service network on land and in the air. The picture shows SF Express Aviation Base at Shenzhen Baoan International Airport in Guangdong Province in the night.

中国快递

干线路由 纵横交错
Trunk Routes - Intersecting and Crisscrossing

　　干线路由构成了快递网络的骨架，它们是贯穿南北、横跨东西的动脉，将不同的转运中心紧密相连，畅通高效地将包裹从一个地方迅速输送至另一个地方，为快递网络提供源源不断的动力。高速公路上货车疾驰，铁路线上货物专列飞奔，深邃夜空中飞机翱翔，交通大动脉纵横交错、四通八达，干线路由交织世界，通达远方。

Trunk routes constitute the skeleton of the express delivery network. They are the arteries that traverse north to south and east to west, seamlessly interlinking various transfer centers. They facilitate the swift and efficient delivery of parcels from one destination to another, pumping a relentless flow of energy into the express delivery network. Trucks race along the expressways, freight trains thunder along the railways, and planes soar in the deep night sky. These transport arteries crisscross and radiate in all directions, and trunk routes not only bridge the world but also stretch its reach far and wide.

快递中国：无远弗届

▲ 航空运输是中国快递网络发达高效的重要支撑。图为中国邮政大型宽体货机执飞"广州—东京"往返航线。
Air transport plays an important role in supporting the sound and efficient functioning of China's express delivery network. The picture shows China Post's large wide-body freighter flying on the "Guangzhou-Tokyo" route.

◀ 在中国，哪里有需要，邮政快递服务就提供到哪里。图为中国邮政车辆行驶在新疆博尔塔拉蒙古自治州。
Where there is a need, there are postal courier services available. The picture shows China Post's long-haul vehicles driving in Bortala Mongolian Autonomous Prefecture, Xinjiang Uygur Autonomous Region.

中 国 快 递

▲ 持续完善的航空运输网络正在提供巨大动能，助力快递物流"加速跑"。图为圆通速递在嘉兴的东方天地港。
The ever-improving air transportation network is providing a huge boost to the acceleration of express logistics. The picture shows the architectural rendering of Dongfang Tiandi Port of YTO Express in Jiaxing City.

▶ 建立航空枢纽、引进先进技术等方式将推动中国快递业向更高水平发展。图为鄂州花湖国际机场。
Establishing aviation hubs and introducing advanced technologies will take China's express delivery industry to a higher level. The picture shows Ezhou Huahu International Airport.

▼ 陆路干线运输是中国快递网络四通八达的坚实保证。图为中通快递干线车辆行驶在新疆赛里木湖畔。
Ground long-haul transportation provides a strong guarantee for the accessibility of China's express delivery network. The picture shows ZTO Express' long-haul vehicles traveling along the shores of Sailimu Lake in Xinjiang Uygur Autonomous Region.

▲ 无论黎明或黄昏,中国快递 24 小时奔流不息。图为韵达速递货车行驶在广袤的草原上。
At dawn or dusk, China's express delivery operates around the clock. The picture shows Yunda Express' truck driving on the vast grassland.

◀ 货运班列不停奔跑，在连点成线、织线成网中保障了铁路国际运邮的需求。图为中欧班列（郑州）运邮顺利开行。
Freight trains keep running non-stop, connecting dots into lines and weaving lines into networks to serve the demand for international transportation of mail by railway. The picture shows the successful launch of CR Express (Zhengzhou) for international transportation of mail by railway.

▼ 高铁以其高速、稳定的运输特点，加入承担快件运输重任的队列中。图为高铁快件整装待发。
High-speed railway, with its unparalleled speed and stability, has joined the community of transporting express shipments. The picture shows a high-speed train fully loaded with express shipments ready for departure.

中国快递 | EXPRESS IN CHINA

末端 星罗棋布
Terminal Outlets - Spreading Across the Country

EXPRESS CHINA – EXTENDING TO EVERY CORNER　　　　　　　　　　　　　　　　　　　　　　　　　　快递中国：无远弗届

　　末端网点是快递网络的神经末梢，密布如星辰，点亮每一座城市、每一个村落。无论是繁华的都市中心，还是偏远的山村角落，快递服务都已深深扎根。小至便利店的一隅，大至专业的服务中心，它们构成了快递网络的毛细血管，让服务无所不在。在这里，每一次包裹的流转，都充满了温情与关怀，每一次送达，都传递着希望与期待。

The terminal outlets are the nerve endings of the express delivery network, spreading across the country and illuminating every city and village. Whether it is a bustling city center or a remote corner of a mountainous village, express delivery is present everywhere. From a corner of a convenience store to a professional service center, these outlets form the capillaries of the express delivery network, making services ubiquitous. In this realm, the circulation of every parcel is full of warmth and care, and every delivery conveys hope and expectation.

◀ （左一）快递服务提高城市居民的生活质量，促进城市经济的发展。图为韵达快递员在重庆解放碑商业区派件。
(First from the left) Express delivery services improve the quality of life for urban residents and promote the development of urban economy. The picture shows a deliveryman from Yunda Express delivering express shipments in Jiefangbei CBD, Chongqing City.

◀ （左二）快递服务已经被纳入许多人的新"开门七件事"之中。图为邮车行驶在柳州三江月亮街。
(Second from the left) Receiving express deliveries has been hailed as one of the new seven daily necessities in many people's lives in China. The picture shows the postal vehicle traversing the Moon Street, Sanjiang Dong Autonomous County, Liuzhou City.

▼ 快递服务站作为快递网络的重要组成部分，极大地便利了人们的日常生活。图为上海圆通快递员派送快件到妈妈驿站。
As an important part of express delivery network, express service stations have greatly facilitated people's daily lives. The picture shows a deliveryman from Shanghai YTO Express delivering express shipments to Mom Station.

中国快递 | EXPRESS IN CHINA

▲ 香港作为一个国际金融中心和自由贸易港，拥有高度发达的快递服务体系。图为京东快递在香港街头配送。
Hong Kong, as an international financial center and a free trade port, boasts a sophisticated and well-established express delivery service system. The picture shows a deliveryman from JD Express delivering parcels on the streets of Hong Kong.

◀ 快递在服务民族地区的同时，也在向外传播当地的文化和历史。图为菜鸟快递员在贵州民族地区古村落配送。
While serving ethnic minority areas, express delivery is also spreading local culture and history outward. The picture shows a deliveryman from Cainiao Express delivering parcels to an ancient village in an ethnic minority area in Guizhou Province.

中 国 快 递 | EXPRESS IN CHINA

◀ 通过水运与其他运输方式相结合，快递网点实现沿河地区的快递服务。图为快递员划船派送。
Integrating water transportation with other modes of transportation, express delivery outlets provide services for the areas along the riverbanks. The picture shows a deliveryman delivering shipments by boat.

▶ 快递网点密布中国大、中、小城市的商业区、居民区和工业区。图为中通快递员正在派送。
Express delivery outlets are densely distributed in commercial districts, residential neighborhoods, and industrial zones in large, medium and small cities in China. The picture shows a deliveryman from ZTO Express delivering shipments.

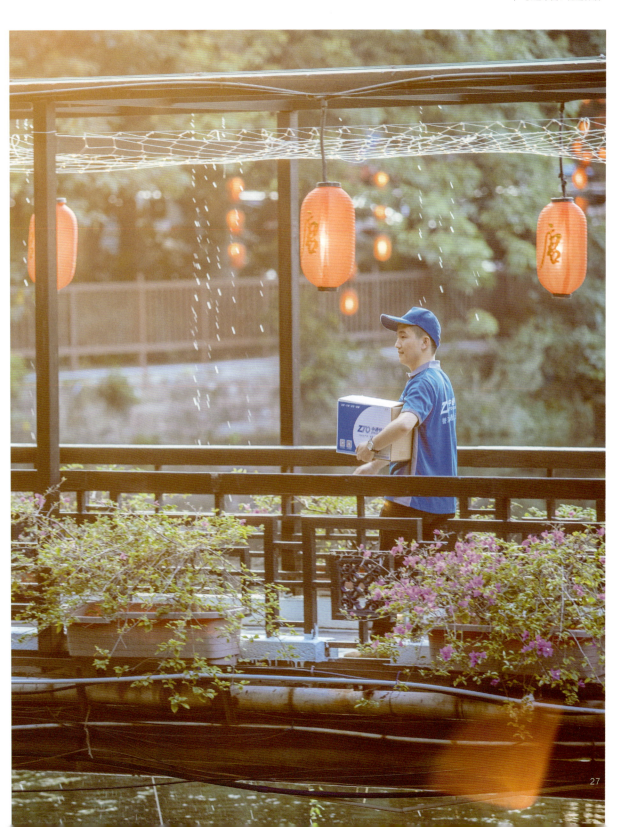

快递是服务生产、促进消费、畅通循环的重要力量。图为京东物流货车穿行在大兴安岭林区。
Express delivery serves as an important force to serve production, promote consumption and boost smooth circulation. The picture shows the trucks of JD Logistics passing through the Daxing'anling forest area.

国际 网络畅联
International - Well-Connected Networks

EXPRESS CHINA – EXTENDING TO EVERY CORNER | 快递中国：无远弗届

中国快递正在跨越国界，与世界紧密相连。海外仓的建立，跨境物流通道的拓宽，国际航班的加密，使得中国商品能够迅速抵达五大洲四大洋，让世界享受到中国快递带来的便利。在这里，每一次快件的流转，都彰显着中国的开放与包容，每一次送达，都传递着友谊与合作。

China's express delivery sector is transcending national boundaries and is closely connected with the world. With the deployment of overseas warehouses, the expansion of cross-border logistics channels and the proliferation of international flights, China's goods can quickly reach their destinations across the world, and the world can enjoy the convenience brought by China's express delivery services. Here, every parcel delivered embodies China's commitment to openness and inclusion, and every delivery conveys a message of friendship and cooperation.

▶ 随着"一带一路"倡议的推进，中国快递公司纷纷加快海外布局。图为顺丰速运在马来西亚提供服务。
With the advancement of the Belt and Road Initiative, Chinese express delivery enterprises have accelerated their overseas expansion. The picture shows SF Express providing services in Malaysia.

◀ 为了提高国际快递效率、降低运营成本，中国快递公司在海外建立仓储和转运中心。图为菜鸟速递在西班牙的转运中心。
To improve the efficiency of international express delivery and reduce operational costs, Chinese express delivery enterprises have established overseas warehouses and transfer centers. The picture shows Cainiao's transfer center in Spain.

▶ 中国快递公司在东南亚的业务发展迅速。图为中通快递柬埔寨金边转运中心。
The business of Chinese express delivery enterprises in Southeast Asia is developing rapidly. The picture shows Phnom Penh Transfer Center of ZTO Express in Cambodia.

▼ 为了更好地适应澳大利亚市场,中国快递公司采取本地化经营策略。图为圆通国际澳大利亚分公司。
To better adapt to the Australian market, Chinese express delivery enterprises adopt the localization strategy. The picture shows the branch of YTO in Australia.

| EXPRESS CHINA – EXTENDING TO EVERY CORNER |

◀ 东南亚是中国快递公司国际化服务的重点区域。图为百世在泰国曼谷的转运中心。
Southeast Asia is the key region in the footprint of international services of Chinese express delivery enterprises. The picture shows BEST's transfer center in Bangkok, Thailand.

▶ 中国快递公司在欧洲的发展是中欧经济合作的重要组成部分。图为京东物流在德国的仓储中心。
The development of Chinese express delivery enterprises in Europe is an important part of China–EU economic cooperation. The picture shows the warehousing center of JD Logistics in Germany.

规模 快速增长
Scale – Rapid Expansion

中国快递着力构建"枢纽+通道+网络"的现代寄递服务网络体系，快递网点基本实现乡镇全覆盖，建制村快递服务覆盖率超95%。截至2023年底，全国拥有快递服务营业网点23.4万处，快递服务网路22.8万条，国内快递专用货机188架，国内快递服务汽车27万辆。中国快递业务量连稳居世界第一。2023年，中国人均快件使用量93.7件，快递支撑网络零售额13万亿元。

China's express delivery strives to build a modern delivery service network and system, characterized by a harmonious integration of "hub + channel + network". Express delivery outlets have basically covered all the towns, and express delivery services have covered more than 95% of administrative villages. Boasting an impressive array of 234,000 express service outlets, 228,000 express delivery routes, 188 freighter aircrafts for express delivery, and 270,000 domestic express delivery vehicles, China has consistently held the top spot globally in terms of express delivery volume for many years. In 2023, China's per capita express delivery volume soared to an impressive 93.7 pieces, and the online retail sales supported by express delivery amounted to ￥13 trillion yuan.

▼ 本节图表数据来源于历年国家统计局统计公报、中国电子商务报告、邮政行业发展统计公报。
Note: The data contained in the figures and charts in this section come from the Statistical Communiques of the National Bureau of Statistics, China Ecommerce Reports, and the Statistical Communiques on the Development of the Postal Industry of the past years.

2014—2023年快递业务量
Express Delivery Volume 2014–2023

(单位：亿件 Unit: 100 million pieces)

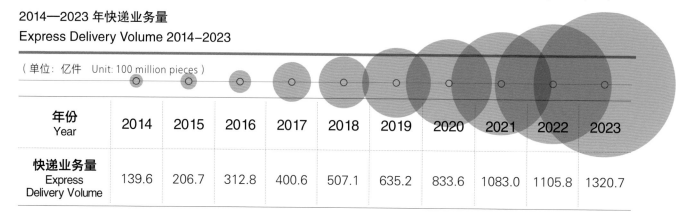

年份 Year	2014	2015	2016	2017	2018	2019	2020	2021	2022	2023
快递业务量 Express Delivery Volume	139.6	206.7	312.8	400.6	507.1	635.2	833.6	1083.0	1105.8	1320.7

2014—2023年快递业务收入和国内生产总值对比
Comparison of Express Delivery Business Revenue and GDP 2014–2023

(单位：亿元 Unit: 100 million yuan)

快递业务收入 Express Delivery Business Revenue	年份 Year	国内生产总值 GDP
12074.0	2023	1260582
10566.7	2022	1204724
10332.3	2021	1149237
8795.4	2020	1013567
7497.8	2019	986515
6038.4	2018	919281
4957.1	2017	820754
3974.4	2016	743585
2769.6	2015	689052
2045.4	2014	635910

▼ 中国快递发展壮大，转运中心逐渐变成庞然大物。图为中通快递在浙江义乌的转运中心。
China's express delivery industry keeps growing and expanding, with transfer centers gradually evolving into behemoths. The picture shows ZTO Express' transfer center in Yiwu City, Zhejiang Province.

2014—2023 年最高日快件处理量
Maximum Daily Express Delivery Volume 2014–2023

（单位：亿件　Unit: 100 million pieces）

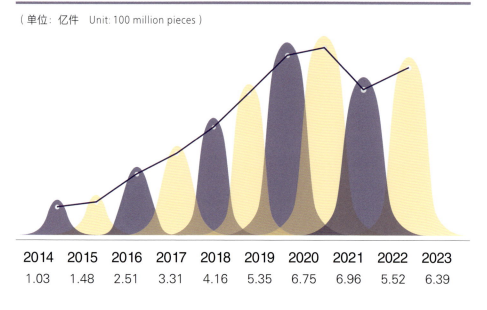

2014	2015	2016	2017	2018	2019	2020	2021	2022	2023
1.03	1.48	2.51	3.31	4.16	5.35	6.75	6.96	5.52	6.39

2014—2023 年国际 / 港澳台快递业务量
International/Hong Kong, Macao and Taiwan Express Delivery Volume 2014–2023

（单位：亿件　Unit: 100 million pieces）

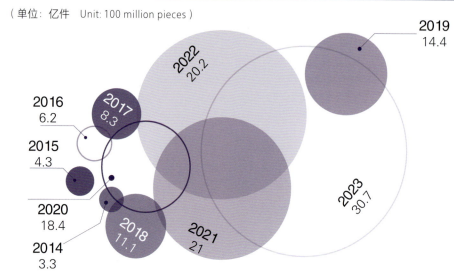

2019 14.4
2022 20.2
2017 8.3
2016 6.2
2015 4.3
2020 18.4
2014 3.3
2018 11.1
2021 21
2023 30.7

2014—2023 年年人均快递使用量
Annual Express Delivery Volume Per Person 2014–2023

（单位：件　Unit: pieces）

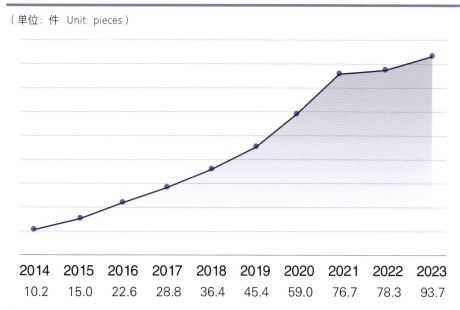

2014	2015	2016	2017	2018	2019	2020	2021	2022	2023
10.2	15.0	22.6	28.8	36.4	45.4	59.0	76.7	78.3	93.7

2014—2023 年支撑网络零售额
Online Retail Sales Supported by Express Delivery 2014–2023

（单位：亿元　Unit: 100 million yuan）

2014	2015	2016	2017	2018	2019	2020	2021	2022	2023
24638	32424	41900	54806	70198.2	85239.5	97590.3	108042	119642	130174

2014—2023 年快递服务营业网点
Number of Express Delivery Service Outlets 2014–2023

（单位：万处　Unit: 10000 pieces）

2014—2023 年网点密度
Density of Outlets 2014–2023

（单位：个　Unit: pieces）

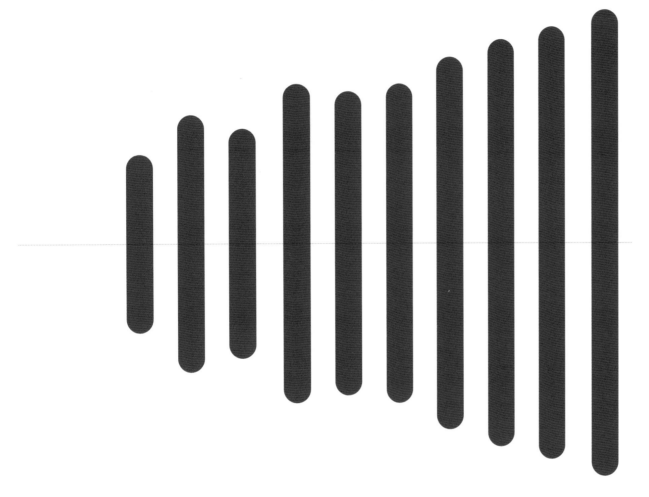

年份 Year	2014	2015	2016	2017	2018	2019	2020	2021	2022	2023
快递服务营业网点数 Number of Express Delivery Service Outlets	13.2	18.3	16.3	21	19.9	21	22.4	22.7	23.1	23.4

每 10 万人网点数（个）Number of Outlets/100,000 Residents	年份 Year	每平方公里网点（个）Number of Outlets/km²
0.00166	2023	0.0244
0.00164	2022	0.0241
0.00161	2021	0.0236
0.00159	2020	0.0233
0.00149	2019	0.0219
0.00142	2018	0.0207
0.00150	2017	0.0219
0.00117	2016	0.0170
0.00132	2015	0.0191
0.00096	2014	0.0138

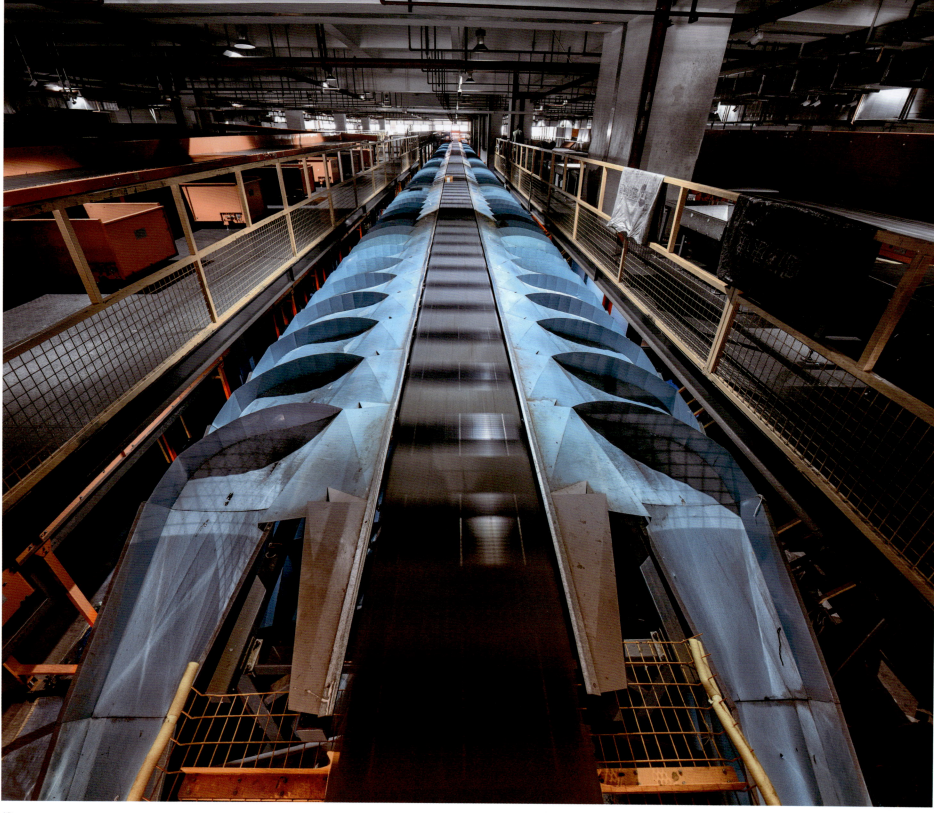

2014—2023 年全国快递服务网路条数
Number of Express Delivery Service Routes 2014–2023

（单位：万条　Unit: 10000 routes）

年份	数量
2014	14
2015	13.4
2016	14.8
2017	20.5
2018	17.7
2019	16.7
2020	20.7
2021	20.0
2022	21.2
2023	22.8

◂ 中国快递公司积极采用先进的信息技术提升服务效率和客户体验。图为充满科技感的转运中心。
Chinese express delivery companies actively adopt advanced information technology to improve service efficiency and customer experience. The picture shows a transfer center filled with a sense of technology.

2014—2023 年国内快递专用货机数量
Number of Freighter Aircrafts for Domestic Express Delivery 2014–2023

（单位：架）

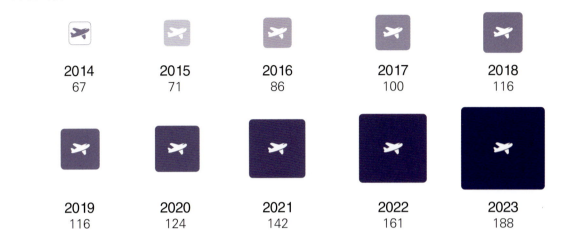

2014	2015	2016	2017	2018
67	71	86	100	116
2019	2020	2021	2022	2023
116	124	142	161	188

2014—2023 年国内快递专用汽车数量
Number of Domestic Express Delivery Service Vehicles 2014–2023

（单位：万辆　Unit: 10000 vehicles）

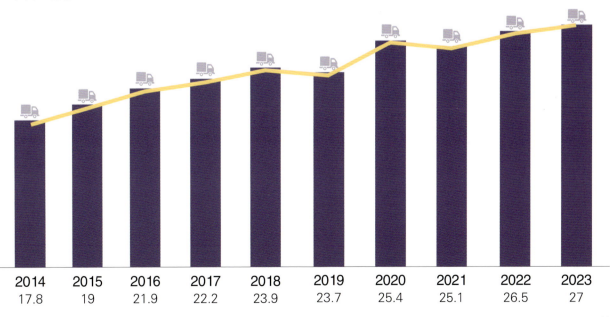

2014	2015	2016	2017	2018	2019	2020	2021	2022	2023
17.8	19	21.9	22.2	23.9	23.7	25.4	25.1	26.5	27

中国快递网点分布广泛，在地理上跨越了山河湖海，在空间上连接了城市乡村。图为邮车行驶在云南罗平的油菜花田。
Express delivery outlets are widely distributed across China, geographically spanning mountains, rivers, lakes and seas and spatially connecting cities and villages. The picture shows the postal vehicle driving through rapeseed flower fields in Luoping, Yunnan Province.

服务 无处不在
Services – Ubiquitous

中国快递服务质量不断提高。2023年，快递服务公众满意度为84.3分，72小时妥投率为80.97%。2023年，全国重点地区快递服务全程时限为56.42小时。邮政快递业不断提升服务质效，有效地满足了人们对快递服务品质的追求和期待。各地特色产品搭乘快递快车，直达千家万户，递送人民群众触手可及的幸福。

The quality of express delivery services in China is constantly improving. In 2023, the public satisfaction with express delivery

2014—2023年快递服务公众满意度
Public Satisfaction with Express Delivery Services 2014–2023

（单位：分 Unit: points）

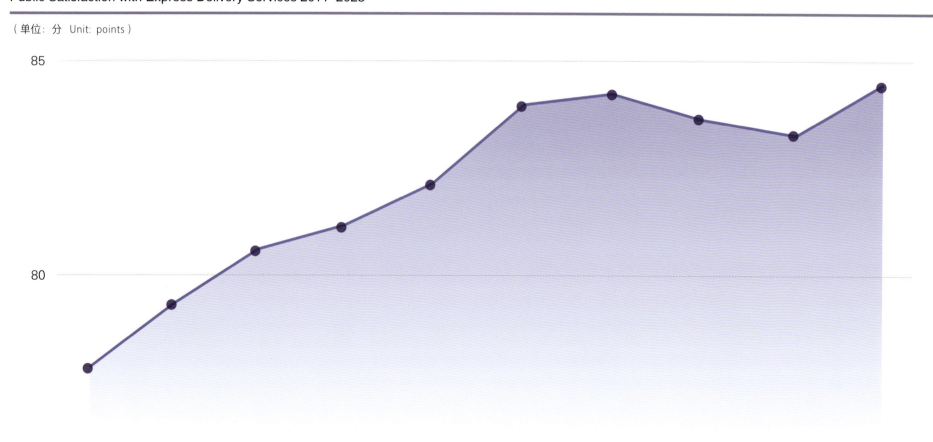

2014	2015	2016	2017	2018	2019	2020	2021	2022	2023
78.4	79.4	80.5	80.8	81.7	84.0	84.2	83.7	83.4	84.3

services was 84.3 points, and the 72-hour delivery rate was 80.97%. In 2023, the end-to-end processing time of express delivery services in key regions in China was 56.42 hours. The postal and express delivery industry has continuously improved the quality and efficiency of its services, effectively meeting people's pursuit and expectations for high-quality services. Local delicacies and specialty products are delivered to doorsteps of millions of households on express delivery vehicles, bringing happiness within reach of the people.

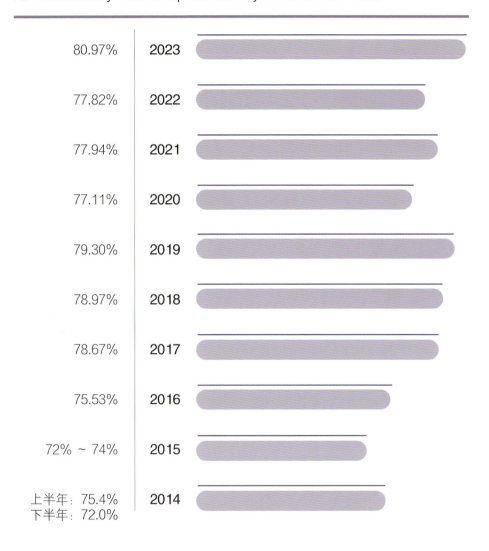

▲ 每次手递手的传递，都为让客户拥有更好的体验。图为农户在蔬菜大棚中接收快递。
Every hand-to-hand delivery is to provide a better experience for customers. The picture shows a farmer receiving a parcel in a vegetable greenhouse.

2014—2023 年快递服务 72 小时妥投率
72-Hour Delivery Rate of Express Delivery Services 2014-2023

Rate	Year
80.97%	2023
77.82%	2022
77.94%	2021
77.11%	2020
79.30%	2019
78.97%	2018
78.67%	2017
75.53%	2016
72% ~ 74%	2015
上半年：75.4% / 下半年：72.0%	2014

▲ 数据来源于历年快递市场监管报告。
Note: The data come from the reports on express delivery market regulation over the years.

◀ 中国快递公司提供了多种客户服务渠道，方便客户咨询和解决问题。图为韵达快递客服中心工作人员。
Chinese express delivery enterprises provide multiple customer service channels to facilitate customers to make inquiries and resolve problems. The picture shows the staff at Yunda Express Customer Service Center.

▶ 快递已经逐渐由一种单纯的物流方式，变为人民群众既用得起、又用得好的生活方式和消费习惯。图为中通快递员在西藏日喀则派送快件。
Express delivery has gradually evolved from a simple logistics mode to an integral part of people's lifestyles and a ubiquitous consumption habit, accessible and embraced by a wide range of individuals. The picture shows a deliveryman from ZTO Express delivering parcels in Shigatse City, Xizang Autonomous Region.

EXPRESS IN CHINA

中 国 快 递

和合融通：万物繁盛
Harmony and Integration – Prosperity for All

满足用户要求，创造用户需求
Meet User Requirements and Create User Needs

一头连着消费，一头连着生产，快递畅通到村促进农村消费增长的同时，更让乡村特色农产品加速"出圈"。图为中通快递在四川眉山正山口村揽收爱媛橙。
Express delivery acts as a vital bridge, linking consumption at one end and production at the other. Extending express delivery services to villages not only spurs the growth of rural consumption, but also accelerates the flow of rural specialty agricultural products into urban market. The picture shows ZTO Express collecting Aiyuan mandarin oranges in Zhengshankou Village, Meishan City, Sichuan Province.

引 言

INTRODUCTION

　　山河辽阔，无需轻舟，自越万山。人们熙来攘往，走过山川湖海；快件东走西进，踏进街巷阡陌，快递业正在更加积极地拥抱新场景、新业态、新趋势。在全球各地、在四面八方、在晨曦日暮，时代的发展、人潮的涌动、情感的温度、效率的极致，在快递中呈现出具体的样貌。

　　花，有一万种开法。从都市繁华到乡村地畔，从百姓家门到工厂腹地，从单一配送到多元化发展，从一个环境过渡到另一个环境，从一个态势抵至另一个态势，中国快递时刻保持着敏锐和果断的决策能力。与城市农村、与生产生活、与社会文明彼此相连，前所未有的生机与活力正在乡村焕发，制造业的运营效率和市场竞争力持续刷新，一个民族最动人的精神底色愈加光亮。

　　果，有四季长和四时香。从少到多，由小及大，由多到更多，中国快递随着时代浪潮迎头向上奔流入海，踏着命运节拍奋勇展臂一往无前，串联着更多场景，展现中国式现代化发展的万千气象，折射出中国的信心和力量，见证着中国经济航船行稳致远。打通城乡双向奔赴的融合之路，激活新消费业态全链条活力，服务全球最具潜力的市场和制造基地，"物畅其流"加速成为现实。

　　心，灿烂而哗然。从一个行业到一个标志，从一个城市到多个国家，中国快递已从最初的商业服务发展为推动经济运行、增强内生动力、服务民生所需的重要力量。商品大流通、生产大发展、文化大繁荣，与千家万户的幸福生活相连，与千城百业的欣欣向荣相承，与世代相传的璀璨文明相接，承载着最为光荣的使命，志在高远，步履不停。

　　中国快递，促进和合融通。

Amidst the grandeur and expanse of mountains and rivers, we remain unfettered, traversing their vastness with ease, without the necessity of a guiding light boat. People come and go, walking through mountains, rivers, lakes and seas; while express packages travel east and west, from bustling streets to remote villages. The express delivery industry is vigorously embracing new scenarios, new formats, and new trends. Across the globe, in all directions, from dawn to dusk, the development of the times, the surge of people, the warmth of emotions, and the relentless pursuit of efficiency all find tangible expression in the realm of express delivery.

Flowers bloom in countless ways. From the vibrant metropolis to the tranquil countryside, from humble households to central areas of industrial factories, from singular delivery services to diversified operations, from one environment to another, and from one context to another, China's express delivery industry maintains its agility to navigate complex market environments with swiftness and precision all the times. This industry, a symphony of urban-rural connectivity, production-life harmony, and societal advancement, breathes new life into rural landscapes, fostering unparalleled vitality and rejuvenation, and enhancing the operational efficiency and market competitiveness of the manufacturing sector, while shining a spotlight on the most profound and touching spiritual essence of our nation.

Fruits bear throughout the four seasons, each with its unique fragrance. From less to more, from small to big, and from abundant to even more abundant, China's express delivery industry rides the crest of the times, plunging into the vast ocean of opportunity with open arms and guided by the rhythm of destiny. It connects numerous scenarios, showcasing the myriad facets of China's modernization development, reflecting China's confidence and strength, and standing as a testament to the steady and far-reaching voyage of China's economic ship. It blazes a trail for urban-rural integration, invigorating the entire ecosystem of new consumption formats, serving the world's most promising markets and manufacturing hubs, and accelerating the realization of "smooth flow of goods".

We stand in awe of the monumental transformation of the express delivery industry. From an industry to a symbol, from operation in one city to the expansion to countries around the world, from a humble beginning as a simple commercial service, it has developed into a pivotal force driving economic operations, bolstering internal growth momentum, and fulfilling the essential needs of people's livelihoods. The massive circulation of goods, the robust expansion of production, and the flourishing of cultural exchanges are all intricately linked to the well-being of countless households, the prosperity of diverse industries across cities, and the resplendent civilization passed down through generations. This industry carries the most noble mission and strides forward relentlessly to achieve lofty goals.

China's express promotes harmony and Integration.

服务乡村 双向奔赴
Serving Rural Areas - Mutual Development

田野间、硕果累、农人笑，小哥跑……橙红橘绿与繁忙寄递交织，诉说着快递与乡村之间的深情厚谊。稳岗就业、精准帮扶，进村小快递，激发大市场，快递全面参与脱贫攻坚战；完善设施、共享成果、嵌入产业链，赋能供应链，快件绘就乡村振兴新面貌；农品直播、畅销内外，按下快进键，跑出加速度，快递促进农村产业结构调整。

Amid lush fields, where harvests abound and farmers smile, the swift movement of deliverymen weaves a tale of profound bond between express delivery and the countryside. By stabilizing employment and providing targeted assistance, small parcels ignite vast markets, with express delivery engaging in the battle against poverty. By enhancing facilities, sharing achievements, embedding into industrial chains, and empowering supply chains, express delivery services paint a new landscape of rural revitalization. With the advent of livestreaming, agricultural products sell well both domestically and internationally; while express delivery accelerates the pace of rural industrial restructuring.

▶ 为提升生鲜寄递时效和质量，快递公司将服务延伸至田间地头。图为申通快递小哥帮农户打包杏，准备收寄。
To improve the timeliness and quality of fresh produce delivery, express delivery enterprises extend their services to the fields. The picture shows a deliveryman from ZTO Express helping farmers pack apricots ready for shipping.

◀ 邮政快递业加速与旅游业融合发展，更好助力乡村振兴。图为安徽黟县邮政分公司揽投员服务宏村游客。
The postal and express delivery industry accelerates its integration with tourism, further boosting rural revitalization. The picture shows a postman from Yi County Post Branch, Anhui Province serving tourists in Hongcun Village.

▼ 快递下乡进村，让偏远地区的农户也能搭上电商快车。图为中通快递员在新疆喀什农户家揽收网销的石榴。
Extending express delivery services to towns and village enables farmers in remote areas to ride the e-commerce express train. The picture shows a ZTO Express deliveryman collecting pomegranates for online sales from a farmer's home in Kashi City, Xinjiang Uygur Autonomous Region.

▲ 快递已经成为农产品进城的重要渠道之一。图为顺丰快递员正在苹果园里揽收快件。
Express delivery has become one of the important avenues for agricultural products to enter cities. The picture shows a SF Express deliveryman collecting parcels in an apple orchard.

▶ （右一）快递服务网络下沉到村，让农产品出村进城更为便捷。图为圆通快递员为当地农产品提供快递运输一体化物流服务。
(First from the right) The extension of express service networks to villages makes it more convenient for agricultural products to enter cities. The picture shows the YTO Express deliveryman providing express delivery and transportation integrated logistics services for local agricultural products.

▶ （右二）越来越多的地方农特产品通过快递渠道走出大山，销往各地。图为德邦快递员在茶园进行现场揽收。
(Second from the right) More and more local agricultural specialties are transported out of mountains through express delivery channels and sold nationwide. The picture shows the Deppon Express deliveryman collecting parcels on-site at a tea garden.

上千个转运中心支撑起中国快递庞大的分拣体量。图为圆通速递安徽芜湖转运中心外景。
Thousands of transfer centers support the huge sorting volume of China's express delivery industry. The picture shows the exterior of the YTO Express Wuhu Transfer Center in Anhui Province.

服务产业 质效双升
Serving Industries - Enhancing Quality and Efficiency

| 和合融通：万物繁盛

减时间、保交付、清库存、降成本、增实力……流水作业与金属交鸣，轻奏出快递业深度服务制造业的生动场景。提高制造业运营效率，提供更加便捷的服务体验，降低供应链风险，增强制造业实力，当快递业用技术创新和数字化转型提供出一站式供应链解决方案，增注的不仅是快递业发展的新动能，更是在刷新制造业的运营效率和市场竞争力。

Reducing time, ensuring delivery, clearing inventory, cutting costs, and bolstering strength…the harmonious symphony of collaboration and coordination between express delivery and manufacturing illustrates the deep integration of the express delivery industry with manufacturing. Boosting manufacturing operational efficiency, providing more convenient service experiences, mitigating supply chain risks, and strengthening manufacturing prowess… the express delivery industry, by leveraging technological innovations and digital transformations, offers one-stop supply chain solutions, not only propelling its own growth with renewed vigor, but also revamping operational efficiency and market competitiveness of the manufacturing industry.

◀ 中国邮政快递业正加速与现代制造业融合发展。图为菜鸟速递为汇川汽车零件厂打造的智慧物流仓储车间。
China's postal and express delivery industry is accelerating its integration with modern manufacturing. The picture shows a smart logistics warehouse built by Cainiao Express for Huichuan Auto Parts Factory.

◀ 快递公司积极布局仓配网络，帮助家装行业解决物流配送难题。图为菜鸟佛山家装仓。
Express delivery enterprises actively deploy warehouse and distribution networks to address logistics and distribution challenges faced by the home furnishing industry. The picture shows Cainiao Foshan Home Furnishing Warehouse.

▼ 快递业通过创新服务为制造产业赋能，助力企业降本增效。图为中邮物流工作人员正在进行冰箱后背板组装工作。
The express delivery industry empowers the manufacturing industry through innovative services, helping enterprises reduce costs and increase efficiency. The picture shows the logistics staff of China Postal Logistics Co., Ltd. (CNPL) assembling back panels of refrigerators.

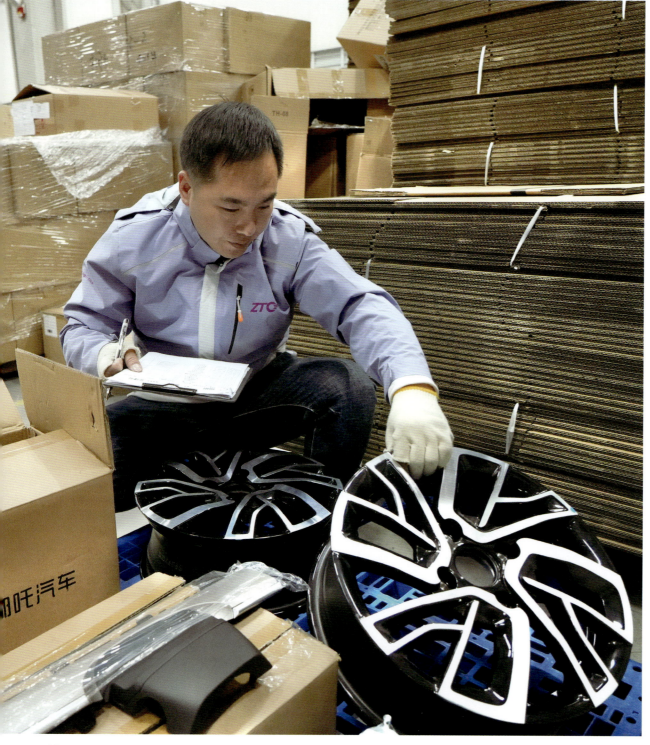

◀ （左一）快递公司加速向综合物流服务供应商转型。图为中通快递员正在为新能源汽车企业提供服务。
(First from the left) Express delivery enterprises are accelerating their transformation to integrated logistics service providers. The picture shows a ZTO Express deliveryman providing services for a new energy vehicle manufacturer.

◀ （左二）快递为城市商家提供包含销售、仓储、发运、配送的一站式仓配一体多级时效履约服务。图为顺丰速运廊坊"上仓下转"仓。
(Second from the left) Express delivery enterprises provide urban merchants with one-stop warehousing, distribution, and fulfillment services with multi-tiered timelines. The picture shows SF Express' new integrated warehouse in Langfang City.

▶ 快递公司进厂驻点提供"一揽子"服务，助力客户寄递无忧。图为韵达快递员在牛奶生产厂家仓库进行揽收。
Express delivery enterprises enter factories to provide a portfolio of services on-site, ensuring hassle-free shipping for customers. The picture shows a Yunda Express deliveryman collecting parcels in the warehouse of the milk manufacturer.

中国快递服务链条在广袤的土地上不断延伸。图为行驶中的韵达快递长途班线车。
The express service chain continues to extend across the vast land of China. The picture shows a long-haul truck from Yunda Express on road.

服务社会 迭代升级
Serving Society - Iterative Upgrades

拓市场、保赛事、增实力、促循环……山川湖海与人群欢叫呼应，传递着中国经济的强劲脉动。点到线、线到面、串珠成链，小小快递在人山人海、摩肩接踵中传送出中国人奋力向前走的印记；全面方案、专项运输、高效稳定，快递让文明薪火相传生生不息；更快、更强、更高，快递人和运动员在体育赛场上找到新的契合点。

Expanding markets, supporting sport events, bolstering strength, promoting circulation…the cheers of jubilant crowds reverberate across mountains, rivers, lakes, and seas, and their interplay resonates with the strong pulse of China's economic vitality. From dot to line, line to plane, eventually forming a cohesive chain, tiny parcels traverse the bustling landscape, embodying the Chinese people's relentless pursuit for progress. With integrated solutions, specialized transportation, unparalleled efficiency, and strong stability, express delivery acts as a beacon, carrying forward the torch of civilization. Just as athletes in the sports arena relentlessly pursue speed, strength, and excellence, so too do the dedicated deliverymen, embodying the same spirit of perseverance and dedication as they both strive for faster, stronger, and higher.

◀ 快递公司发挥自身优势，探索通过直播带货方式助农增收。图为申通快递通过行业媒体直播间帮助江西赣州果农销售脐橙。
Express delivery enterprises, based on their strengths, explore livestreaming sales to increase farmers' income. The picture shows STO Express helping fruit farmers in Ganzhou City, Jiangxi Province sell navel oranges in livestreaming rooms of industry media.

▶ 快递公司充分利用仓网资源，助力电商网络销售。图为菜鸟南宁家电仓员工正在进行装卸作业。
Express delivery enterprises fully utilize warehousing resources to support e-commerce sales. The picture shows the employees of Cainiao Nanning Home Appliance Warehouse conducting loading and unloading operations.

◀ 中国快递公司逐渐成为国际体育赛事上的"常客"。图为在北京冬奥会场馆服务的京东物流无人车。
Chinese express delivery enterprises have gradually become regular participants in international sports events. The picture shows a JD Logistics autonomous delivery vehicle serving at the venues of the Beijing Winter Olympics.

▼ 综合性大型国际体育赛事的物流保障，是对快递公司综合能力的检验。图为圆通速递亚运服务中心。
The logistics guarantee for comprehensive large-scale international sports events is a test of the comprehensive ability of an express delivery enterprise. The picture shows YTO Express Asian Games Service Center.

▲ 随着中国快递公司服务能力的提升，其运输对象从常规货物拓宽至特种货物。图为顺丰速运运输大熊猫香香回国。
With the improvement of the service capabilities of Chinese express delivery enterprises, their transportation objects have expanded from conventional goods to special goods. The picture shows SF Express transporting the giant panda "Xiang Xiang" back to China.

▶ 快递公司用绿色、科技助力赛事物流保障工作。图为京东快递员在"相约北京"系列测试赛现场搬运物资。
Express delivery enterprises leverage green technology to provide logistics guarantee for sports events. The picture shows JD Express deliverymen carrying materials at the "Meet in Beijing" series of test events.

◀ （左一）中国快递串联多元场景，展现中国式现代化发展的万千气象。图为菜鸟上海冷链仓内工作人员正在打包。
(First from the left) China's express delivery connects diverse scenarios, showcasing the myriad facets of China's modernization development. The picture shows a packaging scenario inside Cainiao's cold chain warehouse in Shanghai City.

◀ （左二）快递无人机血液运输航路的开通，为快速、精准、安全配送医疗急救所需血浆提供了便利。图为顺丰无人机在运送血浆。
(Second from the left) The opening of blood transportation routes by express delivery drones has facilitated rapid, precise, and safe delivery of plasma required for medical emergencies. The picture shows a SF Express drone transporting plasma.

中 国 快 递

服务就业 民生之本
Serving Employment - Foundation of People's Livelihood

　　头顶星空，深植厚壤。在经济全球化链条加快重塑、中国经济持续回暖向好、物流技术不断进步的背景下，中国快递蓬勃发展，创造了大量直接和间接的就业机会，为不同技能的劳动者提供了更多就业岗位。收派、分拣、管理、客服……在快递的舞台上，各类型人才如同璀璨星辰，共同织就了一张覆盖城市乡村、连接千家万户的服务网络。他们是这个快速变化时代不可或缺的螺丝钉，共同保障了民生，满足了社会发展的需求，是社会进步的推动者。他们是勤劳的小蜜蜂，起早贪黑，风雨无阻，是最辛勤的劳动者，是美好生活的创造者和守护者，为大家的生活带来便利。

Under the starry sky and deeply rooted in the fertile soil, China's express delivery industry has flourished amidst the accelerated reshaping of the economic globalization landscape, and the sustained recovery of China's economy, coupled with the relentless advancement of logistics technology. This remarkable growth has generated a vast number of direct and indirect job opportunities, thereby providing a broader spectrum of employment avenues for workers with diverse skill sets. From delivery, sorting, management, to customer service… on the stage of express delivery, talents of all stripes shine like bright stars, collectively weaving a service network that spans urban and rural areas and connects millions of households. They are an indispensable component in this fast-changing era, jointly safeguarding people's livelihoods, fulfilling social development needs, and driving social progress forward. The express deliverymen are hard-working little bees, working from dawn to dusk, rain or shine. They are the most diligent workers, the creators and guardians of a better life, bringing convenience to everyone's life.

▶ 快递员等基层一线从业者越来越受到社会的尊重与认可。图为 2019 年快递小哥亮相庆祝中华人民共和国成立 70 周年群众游行方阵。
　 The first-line practitioners, such as deliverymen, are increasingly respected and recognized by society. The picture shows express deliverymen participating in the mass parade celebrating the 70th anniversary of the founding of the People's Republic of China in 2019.

中国快递 | EXPRESS IN CHINA

◀ （左一）通过构建广大的网络，快递带动了偏远地区的就业。图为在西藏日喀则，中通快递小哥正在送货。
(First from the left) By building an extensive network, express delivery has boosted employment in remote areas. The picture shows a ZTO Express deliveryman making a delivery in Shigatse City, Xizang Autonomous Region.

◀ （左二）快递提供了学习和提升技能的机会，助力个人职业成长和长远发展。图为顺丰小哥正在送货。
(Second from the left) Express delivery provides opportunities for learning and skill enhancement, contributing to personal career advancement and long-term development. The picture shows a SF Express deliveryman making a delivery.

➤ （右一）中国快递积极履行社会责任，为残障人士等群体提供就业机会，更好实现人生价值。图为圆通"圆梦行动"残疾员工演唱歌曲《一起向未来》。
(First from the right) Chinese express delivery enterprises actively fulfill their social responsibilities by providing employment opportunities for people with disabilities and others vulnerable groups, enabling them to realize their life values. The picture shows an employee with disability of YTO Express singing the song "Together for a Shared Future" in "Dream Comes True Initiative".

➤ （右二）图为圆通残疾员工正在妈妈商贸直播间直播。
(Second from the right) The picture shows an employee with disability of YTO Express live-streaming at a Mom Trading livestreaming room.

EXPRESS IN CHINA

中 国 快 递

时代命题：美好日长
Era Proposition – Promising Prospects

大道致远，做时间的朋友
Great Path Leads to Vast Distances,
and Be a Friend of Time

每一分钟都是出发,每一步里程都为抵达。图为申通快递车辆行驶在绿色乡间。
Every minute marks a new departure, and every small step leads to arrival. The picture shows a STO Express vehicle traversing through a verdant countryside.

引 言

INTRODUCTION

乾坤有序，万物更迭。创新、协调、绿色、开放、共享正成为开启中国快递高质量发展之门的"金钥匙"，中国快递以奋发有为的姿态主动融入和服务构建新发展格局，积极探索参与全球供应链互联互通的有效路径，不断推动高质量发展。

创新成为第一动力。在创新中变革，在变革中提速：加快发展方式、发展动力、发展领域、发展质量变革，努力实现质的有效提升和量的合理增长；加强创新体系和创新能力建设，激发内在活力，挖掘无限潜力；加速智慧快递建设，从"互联网+"的浪潮中脱颖而出，迈向"智能+"的崭新天地。

协调成为内生特点。通过着力锻长板、补短板，持续提升发展的平衡性、协调性和可持续性，增强对社会生态圈、经济产业链连接的柔韧性；通过高效衔接区域协调发展战略，与综合交通协同布局，与关联产业融合发展；通过共建和共治，促进同频共振，形成高质量发展的合力。

绿色成为普遍形态。绿水青山就是金山银山，我们将"绿色快递"融入这片广袤大地的血脉之中，积极构建与绿色理念相契合的法律、标准、政策体系，持续优化运输结构，减少污染排放，让蓝天白云、繁星闪烁成为常态。快递包装的标准化、循环化、减量化、无害化，是我们践行绿色发展的有力举措。共同走好绿色低碳发展之路，建设更加和谐美丽中国。

开放成为必由之路。我们是全球供应链合作的参与者、受益者，也是坚定的维护者、建设者。我们积极拓展海外服务布局，为"一带一路"建设贡献行业智慧。我们稳步建立境外寄递枢纽，积极参与全球行业治理，与全球同行共同致力于安全、畅通、高效和可持续的全球供应链系统建设。在更高水平的开放中，我们与世界相交，与时代相通。

共享成为根本目的。天地之大，黎元为先。中国快递的发展成果已惠及广大人民群众，并将更多惠及全球大众。不断提升市场主体的服务水平和质量，不断让广大消费者共享行业改革发展成果，不断让行业基层员工更加有归属感，更加体面地工作，拥有更多的尊严。让人人尽享行业发展的红利，让个个感受社会进步的力量。

江河是向海的路，每一步都是追逐。
中国快递，创造美好日长。

The universe operates in order, and things change constantly. Innovation, coordination, green, openness, and sharing are becoming the "golden keys" to unlocking the door to high-quality development of China's express delivery industry. With a proactive and enterprising attitude, China's express delivery sector is actively integrating into and serving the new development paradigm, exploring effective paths to participate in interconnected global supply chains, and continuously pursuing high-quality development.

Innovation has become the primary driving force. Through innovation, we seek for transformation, and through transformation, we aim to accelerate progress. We strive to expedite changes in development mode, drivers, fields, and quality, striving for both qualitative improvement and reasonable quantitative growth. We strive to strengthen the innovation system and capabilities, stimulate our inherent vitality and unleash limitless potentials. We strive to accelerate the development of intelligent express delivery, surging ahead on the crest of the "Internet+" wave and venturing into the untapped frontier of "Intelligence+".

Coordination has become an intrinsic hallmark. By improving our strengths and addressing weaknesses, we strive to enhance the balance, coordination, and sustainability of our development, and strengthen the resilience of our linkages with social ecosystems and economic industrial chains. We strive for seamless integration with regional coordination strategies, fostering collaboration with comprehensive transportation networks, and pursuing integrated growth with related industries. Through joint construction and governance, we strive to foster synergies and form a joint force for high-quality development.

Green development has become a universal pursuit. Lucid waters and lush mountains are invaluable assets. We strive to integrate "green express delivery" into the fabric of this vast land, and actively establish legal, standard, and policy frameworks aligned with green concepts. We endeavor to continually optimize transportation structures, reduce pollution and emissions, and make blue skies, white clouds, and twinkling stars an integral part of our life. We embrace standardization, recycling, packaging reduction and use of non-harmful materials for express packaging as powerful measures to practice green development. Together, let's embark on a path of green and low-carbon development, building a more harmonious and beautiful China.

Openness has emerged as the inevitable path. As participants, beneficiaries, and firm defenders and builders of global supply chain cooperation, we actively expand our overseas service footprint, contributing the wisdom of our sector to the Belt and Road Initiative. We steadily establish overseas postal and express hubs, actively participate in global industry governance, and work with global counterparts to build a safe, smooth, efficient, and sustainable global supply chain system. With a higher level of opening up, we intersect seamlessly with the world and keep pace with the times.

Sharing is the fundamental goal. The well-being of the common people remains paramount, no matter how vast the world is. The accomplishments of China's express delivery industry have already benefited the people and will continue to benefit the people worldwide. We continuously enhance the service levels and quality of market players, empowering consumers to share the fruits of industry reform and development. We ensure that employees at the primary level have a stronger sense of belonging, decency, dignity, and pride in their work. We strive to let everyone enjoy the dividends of industry development and feel the power of social progress.

Rivers flow towards the sea, and every step is a pursuit towards the sea.

China's express promotes prospects.

| 中 国 快 递 | EXPRESS IN CHINA

智能引领 各擅胜场
Intelligence-Driven Development – Each Shining in Its Own Way

▼ 中国快递自动化分拣系统应用比例持续增长。图为京东物流自动分拣机器人。
The adoption of automated sorting system in China's express delivery market continues to rise. The picture shows JD Logistics' automated sorting robots.

自动化分拣系统在中国的快递市场已连续多年保持着高速增长态势。自动分拣技术通过应用先进的机械、电子、传感器、人工智能等技术，实现对包裹的高效、准确分拣，不仅提高了包裹分拣的效率和准确性，降低了人工成本，而且能够适应各种复杂环境，为中国快递的智能化、自动化发展提供了有力支持。

The automatic sorting system maintained a fast-growing trend in China's express delivery market for many years. Automatic sorting technology achieves efficient and accurate sorting of parcels by integrating advanced technologies such as mechanics, electronics, sensors, and artificial intelligence, which not only improves the efficiency and accuracy of parcel sorting and reduces labor costs, but also adapts to various complex environments, providing strong support for the intelligent and automated development of China's express delivery industry.

➤ 智能分拣线的高速运转大大降低了人工成本。图为圆通四川成都转运中心内的四层分拣线。
The high-speed operation of the intelligent sorting line greatly reduces the labor cost. The picture shows the four-level sorting assembly line inside YTO Express' transfer center in Chengdu City, Sichuan Province.

◀ 高耸的货架、穿梭的机器……智慧仓储系统让包裹在库房中流动自如。图为菜鸟无人拣货仓。
Tall shelves, shuttle machines...smart warehousing system allows packages to flow freely in the warehouse. The picture shows Cainiao's unmanned sorting warehouse.

▼ 智能分拣系统的运用大幅提升了包裹处理的效率和准确性。图为京东物流北京亚洲一号智能产业园内,"飞狼"机器人正进行货物分拣出库。
The application of intelligent sorting system greatly improves the efficiency and accuracy of parcel processing. The picture shows the Flying Wolf robots sorting goods out of the warehouse in JD Logistics Asia No. 1 Intelligent Industrial Park in Beijing City.

中国快递

▲ 无论清晨或傍晚，无人驾驶的电动货车都能够直接将快件准确送达消费者手中。图为极兔速递无人快递车夜间运行。
At dawn or dusk, unmanned electric vehicles deliver packages directly and accurately to consumers. The picture shows J&T Express' unmanned delivery vehicles operating at night.

▶ 从初现街头到忙碌于大街小巷，无人车以更多元的应用场景"驶入"百姓生活。图为京东快递无人车服务中。
From first appearance on the streets to shuttling through the streets, unmanned vehicles have driven into people's lives with diverse applications. The picture shows JD Express' unmanned vehicle service.

◀ 无人机的使用开辟了快递配送的新天地。图为韵达速递无人机助力杭州余杭区第三人民医院医疗物资运输。
The use of drones opens up new horizons for express delivery. The picture shows Yunda Express' UAV assisting the transportation of medical materials in the Third People's Hospital in Yuhang District, Hangzhou City.

▶ 起降于城市、山间、海岛的无人机改变着传统的快递模式。图为中通速递在用大型通航无人机。
UAVs taking off and landing in cities, mountains and islands are transforming traditional delivery models. The picture shows ZTO Express' large-scale general aviation UAV.

▶ 无人机运输技术在快递行业的应用日益娴熟。图为顺丰支线无人机。
The application of UAV transportation technology in express delivery industry is becoming increasingly mature. The picture shows the SF Express' regional UAV.

以科技为芯,中国快递驰骋在生机勃勃的土地之上。图为极兔速递车辆行驶在甘肃蜿蜒的山间。
China's express delivery industry, powered by technology, thrives across the vibrant land. The picture shows the J&T Express' vehicle navigating through winding mountains in Gansu Province.

创新求变 改革图强
Innovate for Change - Reform for Strength

未来的中国快递更加注重创新求变，将智能科技融入每一个流程环节。想象一下，自动化设备在转运中心高效运作，确保海量包裹精准流转；无人机和无人车穿梭于城乡的广阔天地，将快递服务带入一个全新的"无人时代"；智能机器人在仓库里忙碌，机械臂如同熟练的舞者，快速而精准地分拣着每一件包裹；大数据和人工智能技术则如同智慧的魔法师，为用户量身定制个性化服务，满足不同寄递需求。在这里，创新不仅仅是技术的革新，更是服务理念的升华，它让快递服务更智能、更高效，也更贴近人心。

Looking ahead, China's express delivery industry will place even greater emphasis on innovation and change, and integrate intelligent technology into every process. Imagine automated equipment operating efficiently in transfer centers, ensuring the precise flow of massive parcels; drones and autonomous vehicles traversing the vast expanse of urban and rural areas, ushering in a brand new "unmanned era" for express delivery services; intelligent robots bustling in warehouses, with robotic arms acting like skilled dancers, sorting each package swiftly and accurately; big data and artificial intelligence technologies serving as wise magicians, tailoring personalized services for users and fulfilling diverse delivery needs. Here, innovation is not merely about technological advancements but also an elevation of service concepts, making express delivery services smarter, more efficient, and closer to people's hearts.

◀ 中国快递不断加大对新技术的投入应用，以进一步提高运输效率。图为顺丰无人机。
China's express delivery industry continues to increase investment in the application of new technologies to further improve transportation efficiency. The picture shows SF Express' UAV.

▶ 人工智能、大数据应用场景在中国快递行业深化拓展，已成为优化服务、提高质效的关键。图为圆通速递总部大数据指挥中心。
The deepening and expansion of AI and big data application scenarios in China's express delivery industry have become the key to optimizing services and improving quality and efficiency. The picture shows the big data command center at YTO Express' headquarters.

▼ 中国快递在更广阔的国际赛事舞台上施展身手。图为圆通快递员在亚运物流中心穿着可穿戴外骨骼设备进行大重量货物分拣。
China's express delivery industry showcases its strengths on a broader international stage of sports events. The picture shows a YTO Express deliveryman using wearable exoskeleton equipment to sort heavy goods at the Asian Games Logistics Center.

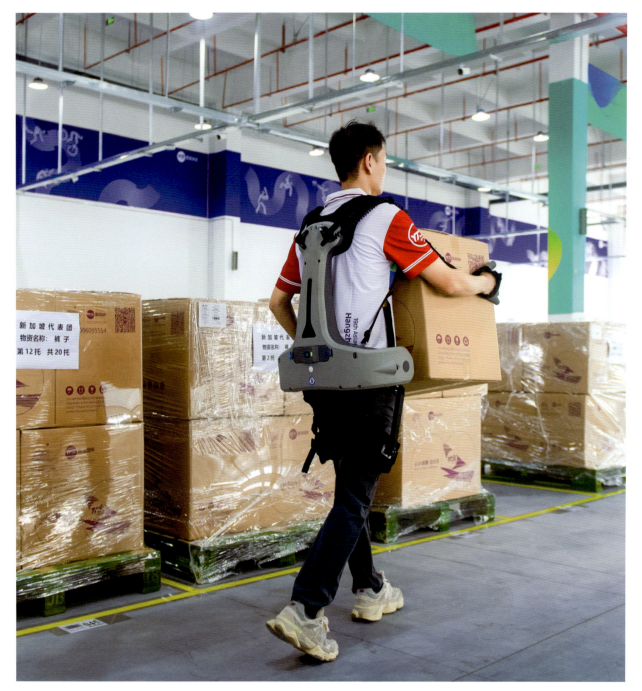

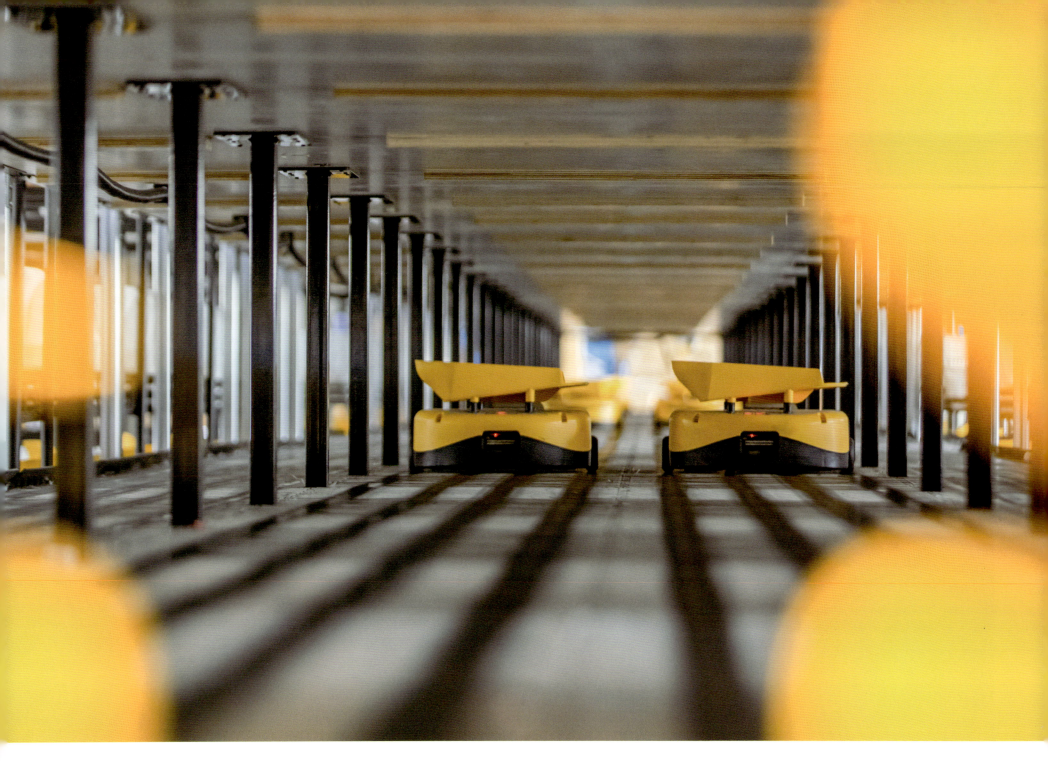

▲ 中国快递不断升级智能分拣等科技装备,生产流程更加智能高效,提升了运营效率。图为菜鸟义乌仓智能分拣机器人。
China's express delivery industry is constantly upgrading technological equipment such as intelligent sorting, making production processes more intelligent and efficient, and improving operational efficiency. The picture shows a smart sorting robot at Cainiao's warehouse in Yiwu City.

◀（左一）无人机技术的广泛运用，为中国快递末端注入活力。图为顺丰无人机助力四川省甘孜州松茸销往全国各地。
(First from the left) The widespread application of UAV technology injects vitality into the last mile delivery. The picture shows a SF Express UAV contributing to the sales of matsutake mushrooms from Ganzi Prefecture, Sichuan Province, to all parts of the country.

◀（左二）无人机可以克服地理障碍，直接将快件送达消费者手中。图为四川省凉山州邮政分公司在昭觉县支尔莫乡"悬崖村"（阿土勒尔村）开通无人机邮路，将"悬崖村"两三个小时的步班邮路缩短为20分钟的"直线升降"。
(Second from the left) UAVs can overcome geographical obstacles and deliver express parcels directly to consumers. The picture shows the Liangshan Prefecture Post Branch in Sichuan Province opening a UAV postal route for "Cliff Village" (Atuleer Village), Zhiermo Town, Zhaojue County, shortening the two-to-three-hour walking journey to a 20-minute "straight-line lifting" journey.

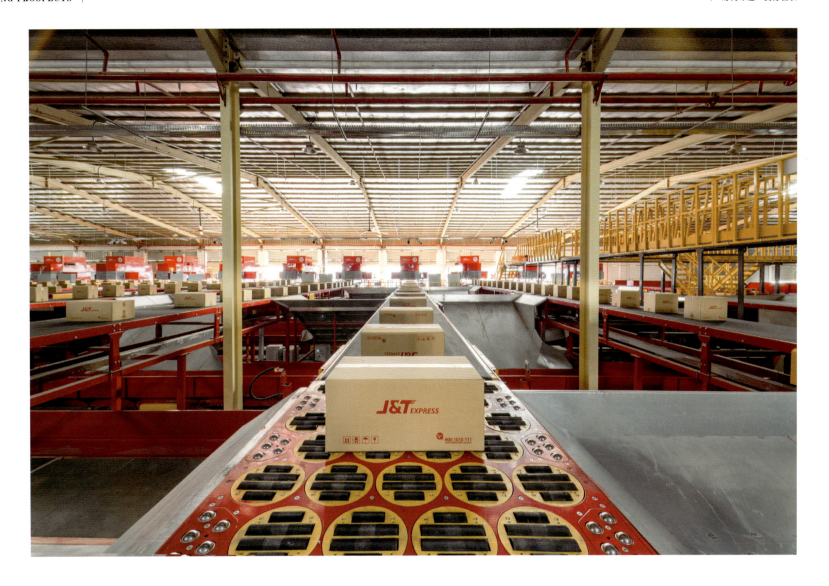

▲ 中国快递的技术、标准、理念受到世界其他国家和地区的欢迎。图为极兔速递沙特阿拉伯的转运中心。
China's express delivery technologies, standards, and concepts are welcomed by other countries and regions around the world. The picture shows the Transfer Center of J&T Express in Saudi Arabia.

◀ 智能快件箱的应用场景不断丰富。图为韵达速递蜜罐智能快递柜进驻上海虹桥火车站，为旅客寄递提供便利。
The application scenarios of smart parcel lockers become more diversified. The picture shows Yunda Express' smart parcel cabinet, "Mi Guan" (literally honeypot) stationed at Shanghai Hongqiao Railway Station, providing convenience for travelers to post and receive parcels.

开放共享 守护美好
Openness and Sharing – Guarding the Future

◀ 中欧班列是推动区域经济发展、加强国际经贸合作的重要平台。2023年6月中欧班列京东号开行。
China Railway Express (CR Express) is an important platform for promoting regional economic development and strengthening international economic and trade cooperation. In June 2023, CR Express JD freight train was launched.

▶ 中国全面开放国内包裹快递市场，推动内外资公平有序竞争，共同分享中国市场这块"蛋糕"。图为UPS在上海世博园开展服务。
China has fully opened up its domestic express delivery market to encourage fair and orderly competition between domestic and foreign investors and share the "cake" of the Chinese market together. The picture shows UPS providing services at the Shanghai World Expo Park.

未来的中国快递更加注重同建共享，坚持普惠民生的理念，让发展成果惠及更多人。中国快递将通过提升服务质量、降低服务成本，让更多消费者享受到便捷、高效的快递服务。共享理念的持续推进，将使资源利用更加合理，无论是城市还是乡村，都能享受到同等的服务。在这里，共享不仅是一种发展模式，更是一种关怀，它让中国快递发展成果惠及每一个人，共同构建一个更加和谐美好的社会。

In the future, China's express delivery industry will prioritize joint construction and sharing, adhering to the principle of inclusive development that benefits the people's livelihood, ensuring that the fruits of development reach broader population. By enhancing service quality and reducing costs, China's express delivery sector aims to provide more consumers with convenient and efficient delivery services. The continuous promotion of the sharing concept will lead to a more rational utilization of resources, ensuring that both urban and rural areas have equitable access to services. Here, sharing is not merely a mode of development, it is also a manifestation of care, enabling the achievements of China's express delivery industry to benefit everyone and contributing to the joint endeavor of building a more harmonious and beautiful society.

▲ 中国开放的姿态吸引了众多国际合作伙伴，与中国快递共同探索新服务、新模式、新技术。图为 DHL 快递在中国开展配送服务。
China's open stance has attracted numerous international partners to jointly explore new services, models, and technologies with Chinese express delivery enterprises. The picture shows DHL Express providing delivery services in China.

▲ 中国快递不断丰富服务品类,让越来越多的人分享行业发展红利。图为圆通快递小哥在商务楼宇派送快件。
Chinese express delivery enterprises continue to enrich their service categories, allowing more and more people to share the dividends of industry development. The picture shows a YTO Express deliveryman delivering parcels in a commercial building.

▲ 中国快递让越来越多的从业者生活得到保障，提升其获得感、幸福感、安全感。图为中通快递为员工举行集体婚礼。
Chinese express delivery enterprises have ensured the livelihoods for an increasing number of employees, enhancing their sense of gain, happiness, and security. The picture shows ZTO Express holding a collective wedding for its employees.

▶ 图为韵达速递在甘肃定西进行助学活动。
The picture shows Yunda Express conducting an Educational Assistance Program in Dingxi City, Gansu Province.

中国快递坚持创新、协调、绿色、开放、共享的新发展理念，不断提升发展水平。图为德邦快递引进的一批高效智能环保运输车辆。
Adhering to the new development concept of innovation, coordination, green, openness, and sharing, Chinese express delivery enterprises are committed to continuous improvement. The picture shows Deppon Express introducing a fleet of efficient, intelligent, and environment-friendly transport vehicles.

只此青绿 山河无垠
Green Sustainable Development – Harmony with Nature

  未来的中国快递更加注重生态环保，积极践行绿色发展理念。快递包装将更多采用环保材料，减少对环境的污染，用另一方式回报自然。运输工具更多采用清洁能源，有效降低碳排放，守护着蓝天白云。快递公司将通过优化运输路线、提高装载率等措施，减少能源消耗。在这里，绿色不仅是对环境的深情呵护，更是对未来负责的担当。绿色快递，将成为中国快递业的一张名片，向世界展示中国在环境保护方面的坚定步伐和卓越成就。

  In the future, China's express delivery industry will place greater emphasis on ecological environmental protection and actively embrace the concept of green development. More eco-friendly materials will be used for express packaging, minimizing environmental pollution and repaying nature in another way. The sector will progressively integrate clean energy sources into its transportation fleet, effectively reducing carbon emissions and safeguarding blue skies and fluffy clouds. Express delivery enterprises aim to reduce energy consumption by optimizing transportation routes, increasing loading rate and adopting other measures. Here, green represents not only a deep love for the environment, but also a solemn pledge to safeguard the future. Green express delivery will become a business card for China's express delivery industry, showcasing to the world China's firm pace and remarkable achievements in environmental protection.

◀ 中国快递绿色包装标准体系逐步完善，多方参与、全链条治理已成共识。图为京东快递员在西藏纳木错使用可循环包装"青流箱"进行配送。
China's green packaging standard system for express delivery is gradually improving, and multi-stakeholder participation and whole-chain management have become a consensus. The picture shows a JD Express' deliveryman using recyclable "Qingliu Boxes" for delivery at Namtso, Xizang Autonomous Region.

▶ 中国快递深化快递包装绿色治理，加快绿色包装的研发和推广，加大绿色低碳科技研发应用。图为顺丰速运研发应用的循环箱"丰·box"。
China's express delivery industry is deepening green governance of express packaging, accelerating the research, development, and promotion of green packaging, and intensifying the research and application of green and low-carbon technologies. The picture shows SF Express' recyclable packaging box – "Feng Box".

◀ 中国快递积极推进分拨中心光伏发电建设，为分拣操作设施提供清洁电力，助力环境可持续发展。图为中通快递在浙江台州转运中心铺设的光伏发电设备。
China's express delivery industry is actively promoting the construction of photovoltaic power generation facilities at distribution centers to provide clean electricity for sorting operations and boost environmentally sustainable development. The picture shows photovoltaic power generation equipment atop ZTO Express' transfer center in Taizhou City, Zhejiang Province.

▼ 图为装备太阳能板的菜鸟武汉快消仓。
The picture shows a Cainiao Fast Moving Consumer Goods (FMCG) warehouse in Wuhan City equipped with solar panels.

◀ 新能源汽车的应用日益增加，推动中国快递实现绿色转型。图为圆通速递新能源厢货服务亚运会。
The increasing adoption of new energy vehicles is driving the green transformation of China's express delivery industry. The picture shows YTO Express' new energy vans serving the Asian Games.

▲ 图为菜鸟杭州保税仓应用的电动汽车。
The picture shows electric vehicles used in Cainiao's bonded warehouse in Hangzhou City.

天高任鸟飞，天阔凭鱼跃，风光无限在未来。一路向前的中国快递驰骋在辽阔大地，不断满足着人民群众日益增长的用邮需求。图为菜鸟速递将快件运输至西部山区。
The sky is high for birds to fly, the sea is vast for fish to leap, and the future holds boundless opportunities. China's express delivery industry is moving forward relentlessly across the vast land, continuously meeting the growing postal needs of the people. The picture shows Cainiao Express delivering parcels to a mountainous region in western China.

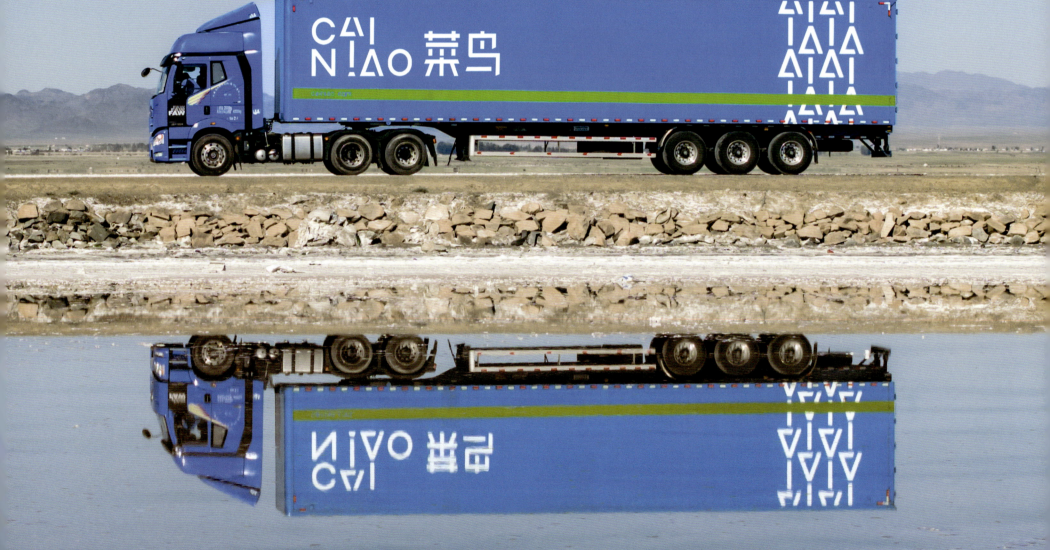

后 记

《中国快递》是中国交通名片丛书之一，由中国邮政快递报社编写。

本书围绕"快递中国：无远弗届""和合融通：万物繁盛""时代命题：美好日长"三大主题，生动展现中国快递行业的非凡成就。

从"年均百亿件"的里程碑，到"月均百亿件"的新常态，这一个个跃动的数字，记录着中国快递的磅礴力量。北斗加持的干线车辆，呼啸而至的飞机高铁，智能升级的快递装备，广泛应用的无人机无人车，用澎湃的创新力量，不断充盈中国快递的无限动能。

在一个个村落，快递进村使村民们富起来的故事不断上演；在一间间工厂，快递与制造业深度融合、降本增效的案例不断迭代；在一座座车站，中欧班列满载货物不断提速……从乡村田野之上，到高楼大厦之间，中国快递的经纬脉络中，涌动着通达四方的奋进能量；无论内循环还是双循环，中国快递用无数次出发与抵达，彰显了连接内外、联通世界的坚定步伐。

多式联运，科学配载；全面电动，先行先试；循环瘦身，光伏并网，逐"绿"而行，驰而不息，续写着因"绿"而兴的壮丽篇章。中国快递的发展成就举世瞩目，已成为全球快递市场发展的坚实基石和澎湃动力。贯通经济大动脉，畅通百姓幸福路，中国快递正加速从"无处不在"迈向"无时不至"的新境界。

在此，我们衷心感谢人民交通出版社的鼎力支持，感谢社领导舒驰、刘韬对书稿的编写提出宝贵意见，何亮、杨丽改、刘捃梁等编辑对本书做了细致的审校工作。你们的辛勤付出，让这本书更加完善。

我们期待，《中国快递》的出版发行，能成为中华人民共和国邮政快递事业发展的珍贵历史记录，让世界各地的读者更加深刻地了解中国快递的速度与活力，共同见证中国从快递大国向快递强国迈进的辉煌历程。

编者
2024年9月

EPILOGUE

"Express in China" is one of the "Card Book Series: Transport in China" and is compiled by China Post and Express News.

This book, focusing on three major themes: "Express China – Extending to Every Corner", "Harmony and Integration – Prosperity for All", and "Era Proposition – Promising Prospects", vividly displays the outstanding achievements of China's express delivery industry.

From "10 billion parcels annually" to "10 billion parcels monthly", the leaping numbers embody the immense potential of China's express delivery industry. Beidou-enabled long-haul vehicles, roaring airplanes and high-speed trains, intelligently upgraded express equipment, and widely used drones and vehicles, continue to drive China's express delivery industry forward, with their surging power of innovation.

In villages, stories of villagers getting rich due to the entry of express delivery to villages keep emerging; in factories, cases of deep integration between express delivery and manufacturing, leading to cost reduction and efficiency improvement, constantly evolve; at railway stations, the speed of China Railway Express trains laden with goods continues to increase... From rural fields to towering skyscrapers, within China's express delivery network, there flows a vibrant energy striving to reach all corners of the world. Whether in the context of domestic circulation or dual circulation, China's express delivery industry, with their repeated departures and arrivals, demonstrates China's firm strides in connecting China with the rest of the world and reaching out to the world.

Multimodal transportation, scientific loading, comprehensive electrification, pioneering trials, circular economy, grid-connected photovoltaic system, and relentless pursuit of environmental sustainability continue to write a beautiful vision of prosperity fueled by "green" initiatives. China's express delivery industry has achieved historic and eye-catching accomplishments, providing a solid foundation and powerful impetus for the development of the global express delivery market. By connecting the "main arteries" of economic development and paving the way for people's happiness, China's express delivery industry is accelerating its transition from being "everywhere" to being "always available".

We would like to express our heartfelt thanks to China Communications Press for its strong support, to its management, Shu Chi and Liu Tao, for their valuable comments on the drafting of the book, and to the editors, He Liang, Yang Ligai and Liu Junliang, for their meticulous review and proofreading of the book. Your diligent efforts have made this book even more complete.

We anticipate that the publication of "Express in China" will serve as a valuable record of the development of the postal and express delivery industry in the People's Republic of China, enabling readers worldwide to gain a deeper understanding of the speed and vitality of China's express delivery industry. Together, let us witness the glorious journey of China's transition from a country with a large express delivery industry to a country with a strong express delivery industry.

Editors
September 2024

图书在版编目（CIP）数据

中国快递：汉文、英文 / 中国邮政快递报社编.
北京：人民交通出版社股份有限公司，2024.9.
ISBN 978-7-114-19725-3

Ⅰ.F632-64

中国国家版本馆CIP数据核字第2024GD2169号

本书由人民交通出版社独家出版发行。未经著作权人书面许可，本书图片及文字任何部分，不得以任何方式和手段进行复制、转载或刊登。版权所有，侵权必究。

Copyright © 2024

All rights reserved. No part of this publication may be reproduced, stored in a retrieval system, or transmitted in any form or by any means, electronic, mechanical, photocopying, recording or otherwise, without the prior written permission of the copyright holder. Printed in China.

Zhongguo Kuaidi

书　　名：	中国快递
著 作 者：	中国邮政快递报社
责任编辑：	何　亮　杨丽改
责任校对：	赵媛媛　卢　弦
责任印制：	刘高彤
出版发行：	人民交通出版社
地　　址：	（100011）北京市朝阳区安定门外外馆斜街3号
网　　址：	http://www.ccpcl.com.cn
销售电话：	（010）85285857
总 经 销：	人民交通出版社发行部
经　　销：	各地新华书店
印　　刷：	北京雅昌艺术印刷有限公司
开　　本：	965×635　1/8
印　　张：	17
字　　数：	168千
版　　次：	2024年9月　第1版
印　　次：	2024年9月　第1次印刷
书　　号：	ISBN 978-7-114-19725-3
定　　价：	328.00元

（有印刷、装订质量问题的图书，由本社负责调换）